My Journey to
FREEDOM

The
Edith
Schubert
Story

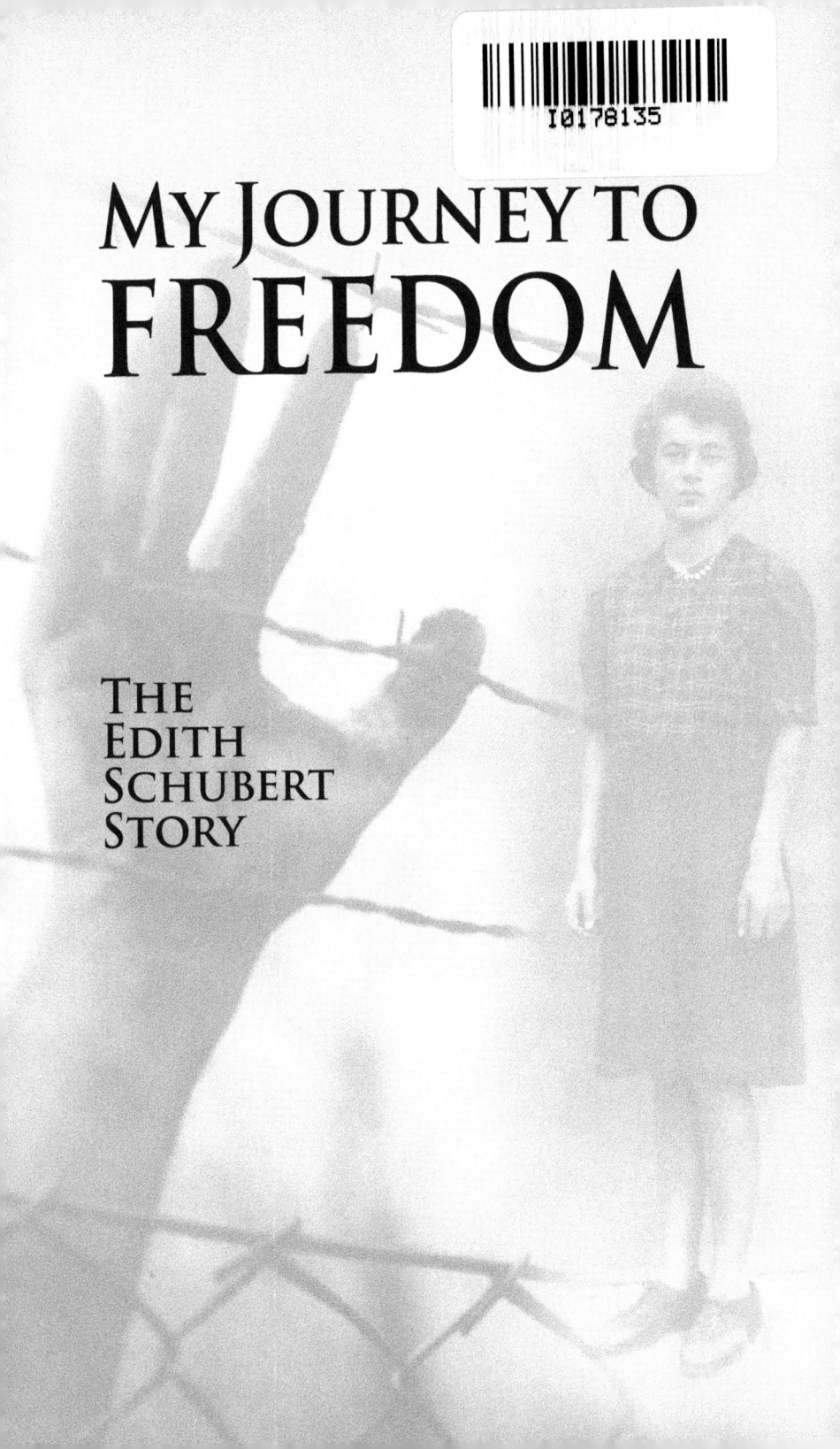

MY JOURNEY TO FREEDOM

THE EDITH SCHUBERT STORY

Edith Schubert Combs

HUNTER ENTERTAINMENT NETWORK

Colorado Springs, Colorado

My Journey to Freedom: The Edith Schubert Story
Copyright ©2018 by Edith Schubert Combs
First Edition: July 2018

To order products, or for any other correspondence:

Hunter Entertainment Network
4164 Austin Bluffs Parkway, Suite 214
Colorado Springs, Colorado 80918
www.hunter-ent-net.com
Tel. (253) 906-2160 – Fax: (719) 528-6359
E-mail: contact@hunter-entertainment.com
Or reach us on Facebook at: Hunter Entertainment Network
"Offering God's Heart to a Dying World"

This book and all other Hunter Entertainment Network™ Hunter Heart Publishing™, and Hunter Heart Kids™ books are available at Christian bookstores and distributors worldwide.

Chief Editor: Gord Dormer
Book cover design: Phil Coles Independent Design
Layout & logos: Exousia Marketing Group www.exousiamg.com
ISBN: 978-1-937741-16-7
Printed in the United States of America.

Dedication

I am dedicating my story with memories to my Mom & Dad, Eduard and Berta, as well as my three sons: Edward, David, and Jeffrey.

Acknowledgments

My story in this book tells it all, but Mrs. Robinson in Rabensburg, Austria saved my life, along with our Father in Heaven.

Table of Contents

*Includes photo layout from Edith's journey

Chapter 1
My Childhood Memories

I was born in Kl. Jestreb, Czechoslovakia on April 26, 1932 to Eduard and Berta Schubert, who named me Edith Maria. I was the second child in a family of four children: Martha, myself, Burkhard, and Helmut.

My early memories began in 1937 when I entered Kindergarten. Because we lived in the small town of Kl. Jestreb, there were not many children in my class. The Kindergarten room didn't have many toys, but all of us had small cots for afternoon naps. There was also a small chapel and a small fire station in our town. About half of the people in the area worked on small farms like my dad's.

I never saw my dad when he wasn't doing something, except on Sunday when we went to church. He got up every morning at five o'clock to do the chores and feed and milk our two cows. Then, he would feed our two pigs and twenty chickens. Dad was also a good writer and knew the law. All of our relatives, plus the townspeople, came to Dad when they needed a letter written to the government. He never turned anyone away. Many times, he would sit up until late at night and write, get a few hours of sleep, and then get up to start a new day.

My mother worked in a factory in Zabre, about three miles from our home. She rode a bicycle to and from work. Martha was in middle school and walked to Zabre five days a week. After school, Mother would be waiting for her with a change of clothes, so she could go directly to work in the fields, where she worked until dark. She did her homework after supper.

I always looked forward to Sunday. We would put on our good clothes, and walk to the next town as a family. After church, we would stop at the cemetery to clean the family graves. After we returned home from church and had dinner, we usually visited our grandparents and other relatives.

In 1938, German Chancellor Adolph Hitler declared war on Poland, where he faced stubborn resistance. The Polish people fought as long as they could, but Hitler's forces outnumbered them with men, as well as weapons. In March, Hitler's army marched into Austria. On October 2, 1938, the German Army marched into Czechoslovakia. Because our family was German, we had to fly a German flag from our house. The night before the invasion, my mother sewed the flag, working on it into the early morning hours. Our house had a small window in the attic facing the front, so Dad found a long pole and secured the flag to it. I was 6 ½ years old.

In protest of the invasion, my dad wrote a letter to Hitler asking him to stop this crazy war. A few days later, we were awakened at 4:00 in the morning by loud voices. All of us children looked out the window and saw two SS soldiers putting chains around my dad's hands and legs, and then they took him away. My mother pleaded with them, telling them that she needed him on the farm, but they showed no kindness and left with him. Six weeks later, my dad was released. I am sure he had learned to keep his thoughts to himself. Dad never joined the Nazi Party, and that was in favor with our Czech neighbors.

Because we spoke German at home, we went to a German school. After the invasion, we had to learn two German hymns, and we began every school day by singing those hymns, raising our right hand while singing. At the beginning of 1940, I remember listening to Hitler talking on the radio, telling the people how strong his army was and that he would conquer the world.

During the winter and spring of 1940, we did not have a lot of work to do on the farm, so my mother had a little more time after work. She made all of us nice outfits for church. I turned eight-years-old in April, and around that time, work began on the farm. My mother believed I was then old enough to work, so after school, I would go straight home, change clothes, and clean the area where the cows were penned, putting down clean straw. I would then take care of the pigs. I also took care of the chickens, penning them up for the night. I don't remember having any toys, but we always had something to do until dark. We then ate supper and did our homework.

After school one day, I wanted to stay and play with some of my schoolmates, although I knew I was supposed to go straight home after school; it felt nice to play with other kids. From where I was playing, I could see the road to our house, and after I had been playing for about an hour, I saw my mother coming. She had a long switch in her hand, the one we used on our cows when they pulled the wagon. She whipped me all the way home. My dad finally stopped her by putting his hands out and holding her, while I stood behind him. I have never forgotten that whipping.

We only had six weeks of school vacation during the summer, so one day in August, my mother decided that she and I would clean the pigpen together. We kept the bales of straw in the barn in the upper loft. We had no stairs for the loft, only a big long ladder. I started to go to the barn, but my mother told me to finish cleaning the pigpen and she would get the bales of straw. Dad kept the wagon he used to bring in the wheat from the fields in the barn. The sides of the wagon had big, wooden spikes. I waited for Mother to come out of the barn, and when she didn't come out, I went to see about her. As I opened the barn door, I saw her on top of those wooden spikes. Then, she fell on the floor. She was crying and in a lot of pain. I saw a big hole in her side, and blood was gushing out. She whispered to me to go get Aunt Mili, so I ran all the way to her house. We were both crying as we ran back to the barn. I was so afraid that my mother might be dead already, but she was still alive. My dad was in Zabre, so someone notified Martha, who was working in the field, and she went to find Dad.

By the time Mother got to the hospital and onto the operating table, three hours had passed. It was a miracle that she had not bled to death, but Aunt Mili had torn up a white sheet and packed it into the hole in Mother's side. That kept Mother from bleeding to death.

Mother survived the surgery and slowly got better. Every Sunday, Dad took us to see her. We walked for an hour to the train station and then rode the train. After three weeks, on a Sunday when we were at the hospital, the doctor told my dad that he could come back in two days to take Mother home. She was sitting up patching our socks and smiling. She could not wait to get home.

Dad took all of us kids to bring Mother home. When we got to the hallway near Mother's room, a doctor met my dad and told him that they had to x-ray Mother one more time to make sure she was healing okay. That is when they found that she was filled with infection. The doctor had to operate on her again. We kids were not allowed to go into Mother's room, but when Dad was leaving her room, we heard Mother say, "Oh, my Edi, I don't want to die." We went home with heavy hearts. The next day, Dad went back to the hospital, and when he came home, he said, "She died in my arms."

Chapter 2
Losing My Mother Was Just the Beginning

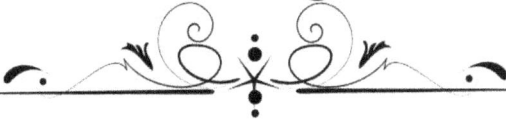

Mother came home in a nice casket. The funeral home hung black drapes around the bedroom and then set up the casket with big candle stands around it. We had Mother for three more days, and I think all of the people from our hometown came to view her. Dad hardly left her room.

On the day of the funeral, the casket was taken to the cemetery by a horse-drawn buggy. The hearse had black drapes and was closed in with glass. It was raining. My cousin Helga and I walked behind the casket and then came the rest of the family, relatives, and friends. It took us about 1 ½ hours to walk to the nearby town of Pobutch. We stopped at the church for the funeral service and then went on to the cemetery. That was the hardest part... the final goodbye. Dad was still in shock. As the casket was lowered into the ground, relatives had to hold Dad back.

With Mother gone and the war going on, we children felt the pinch on the farm. Martha had to quit school and work on the farm with Dad, and about the only cooked meal we had was on

Sunday. We were outgrowing the clothing Mother had sewn for us, and we had to wear hand-me-downs from relatives. The clothes I wore to school always had patches on them, and my shoes were torn. Hitler's order to serve hot meals in all German schools was the best thing that could have happened to my brothers and me. Getting a hot meal meant so much, but that was all I liked about Hitler and the war.

In 1942 when I was ten-years-old, Burkhard and Helmut came down with diphtheria and had to go to Zabre to the hospital. One day, Dad and I walked to Zabre to catch a train to visit my brothers. They were in an isolated ward, which was upstairs in the hospital, so we could only talk with them from downstairs. Both were crying because we could not take them home, and Dad was upset about having to leave them there.

Two days after we returned home, while I was at school, my nose began bleeding really hard. I was sent home. That evening, my throat began to hurt. I was almost sure I had diphtheria, but I begged Dad not to take me to a doctor, because I was afraid of being stuck with a big, long needle in my behind. Dad kept me home and by 4:00 in the morning, I couldn't breathe. I woke Dad and he looked at my throat. My air passage was covered with green and yellow puss, and I was struggling to get air. I thought I was going to die. Dad built a fire in the stove, warmed some saltwater, and told me to gargle. Big lumps of puss came out and my breathing became a little easier, but I was really sick for the rest of the day. Dad had to report my case of diphtheria, so state officials came and embalmed (fumigated) our kitchen. I slowly recovered, and Dad said I was a lucky girl, because children with diphtheria who don't get medical help usually die, so God still had plans for me.

During the summer of 1943, there was always more work time than playtime, but one Sunday afternoon, I wanted to go bicycle riding with a friend. Our family only had one bicycle, which belonged to my mother. After Mother's death, Martha claimed the bicycle, since she was the oldest. I was not allowed to ride the bicycle, so I decided to sneak off. Burkhard and Helmut wanted me to take them for a ride also, so I told them to meet me at the bottom of the hill. I had been riding for about ten minutes when I came to a big curve. I couldn't stop, and a big truck ran over me. I never felt the impact, but I woke up underneath the engine. Everyone thought I was dead, so when I showed signs of life, they pulled me out and laid me on the side of the road. Someone walked to the schoolhouse for a stretcher, while someone else notified my sister. When she arrived at the scene, the first thing she said was, "My poor bike!"

I was carried to a nearby gasthaus where we waited for a doctor to come from the big city with the ambulance. My left leg, which was curled up like a snake, was broken in three places. The doctor pulled my leg straight out, and I let out a bloody yell; the pain was terrible! We had a long drive to the hospital, and my family was told that I might live three more hours. I remember making it to the surgery room. They were cutting my dress off of me, and then I went into a deep sleep. When I woke up, my left leg was up on some kind of track with a large needle through my knee. Attached to that needle was a kind of horseshoe with a small rope that had weights hanging from it. The rope, which went from the needle to the end of my leg, was supposed to keep my leg from getting shorter. I also had internal injuries.

I was in a women's ward with other sick women, and I was the only child. My bed faced the door, so the first thing visitors would see was the bottom of my foot, which was black and as hard as leather from not wearing shoes all summer. The nuns tried to scrub my foot, but that didn't help. Finally, they put a white sock over my foot, and people stopped staring at me.

Dad visited me about every other day so one day, I asked him to bring me German pancakes. The next visit, he brought them. I ate them right away, and before visiting hour was over, my stomach was hurting badly, and I began screaming. All the visitors had to leave the room. My dad was told never to bring me food again; I was on a special diet, because of my internal injuries.

I was in the hospital for four months, and I got to know everyone in that ward. One day, the nuns took me to the next room, which was where my mother had died. The nuns even took me to their chapel to pray. I was in the hospital for six weeks, and then I was in a leg cast for another six weeks. After my cast was removed, I had to learn to walk again. The nuns always looked after me, and when I returned home, I missed them as much as I missed the good food.

Because I was in the hospital for so long, I missed a lot of school, but in time, I slowly made it up. One day in the spring of 1944, four of us girls decided to walk in the woods to look for strawberries. As we approached a bridge, we saw four prisoners of war (POWs) hiding under the bridge. They signaled to us not to say anything to anyone, and we did not tell, but in our town was a mean old man named Mr. Focher. He was always looking for POWs and even deserters from the German army who just wanted to go home to their families. One deserter ran through our hills, and Mr. Focher saw him, ran after him, shot him dead, and dragged him by his feet down the hill to show us townspeople what happens to deserters. Because he worked for the SS, no one dared say anything to him.

The day after we had seen the POWs, we went to school and there stood the four POWs with Mr. Focher, plus other SS men. We children had to stand there and watch the SS men beat the POWs half to death. There were two American soldiers, one French soldier, and one British soldier. After we watched the beating, we were sent back to the classroom. We never learned what happened to the POWs after that.

Chapter 3

The Draft:
Now Without Both Parents

The war was getting worse, and Hitler was getting short on manpower, so he began drafting young boys and sick people like my dad, who was not well enough to be put on the front lines, but Dad was not allowed to stay home. In the summer of 1944, he had to join the army.

In September of 1944, we were tested in school for tuberculosis. Two girls and I tested positive. In the spring of 1945, the government was making plans to send us three girls to the North Sea to a sanitarium. As the time got closer for us to leave, we learned that the Russians had marched into Poland, which was close to the North Sea, so that ended the cure for my tuberculosis. I was getting weaker, but God gave me strength to go on. Without God, I could have never have survived the ordeal I was about to endure. After Dad was drafted, Grandmother Ludmilla Schubert came to live with us, but things did not get better. Martha and my grandmother worked the fields all day, while Burkhard, Helmut, and I went to school. We got a hot meal at school, but as soon as we got home, we had to do our share of work. Food was getting scarce, especially for people who lived in the city. Everything was rationed. When we killed one of our pigs, we had to give the other one to the German Army. We also had to give half of everything grown in the fields to the government free of charge.

In late 1944, the Russian army was getting closer, and the German army was moving back. Then, in February of 1945, the Germans brought many Russian POWs to our neighboring town to spend the night. We could tell the prisoners were very tired from walking all day in the cold. They did not have warm clothing, and we could see the hunger in their faces. Some of us kids ran home and got bread and gave it to some of the POWs.

The Germans boarded the POWs with a few Czech farmers. One family had just killed a pig, and it was hanging on one side of their attic. A stone wall divided the attic, and a bunch of POWs were moved into the other side for the night. The poor men were starving, and they could smell the pig on the other side, so they broke down the wall and ate the pig raw.

The next morning, we children watched the POWs line up for another day's walk. As they walked down the road, we heard a couple of shots. The SS soldiers had killed two of the POWs, because they were too weak to walk.

During March and the beginning of April of 1945, things got worse by the day. The Russians were pushing Germans back, and Hitler was running out of men and food. Our dad was stationed not too far from our home, so he wrote a letter asking Martha to bring him bacon and bread. She borrowed a bicycle and rode to see Dad. I wanted to see Dad as well, so I went to one of the neighbors who had some refugees from Hungary. I begged them to lend me a bicycle and after they heard my story, they let me borrow the bicycle, but I had to return that evening.

My nightmare began when I reached Smole. To my surprise, the main road through the town was full of trucks and tanks moving back from the front line. Suddenly, I heard planes flying really low, and they began shooting at the tanks. There I was, next to the road on the sidewalk pushing my bike. I was so scared. I went to a gasthaus to find shelter, but the people who ran it pushed me outside and called me a German pig. I was so surprised to hear them say that. I had no idea Czechs hated us so much. We and our forefathers had lived with them for hundreds of years.

I was determined to make it to where my dad was and as afraid as I was, I finally made it. Martha was already there, and my dad got a worried look on his face when he saw me. He wondered how I had gotten safely through all the danger on the road. Dad was with a bunch of wounded soldiers, and he shared the food with them that my sister had brought for him.

Martha and I had two hours with Dad, and then we had to leave. We could not ride our bicycles at all. We could hear the fighting from a distance, and for some reason, we had to walk toward Zabre. As we approached Zabre, we saw Germans putting dynamite under a big bridge, so they could blow it up before the

Russians came. We were about three miles from home, so we were able to ride our bicycles the rest of the way.

When we got to our town, we were surprised to see people standing around. They did not know what to do. Some people had already loaded their wagons and fled. Grandmother Schubert said Cousin Elsa and her husband had taken Burkhard and Helmut in a wagon and fled to the hills. Martha went back to town to see what the people were going to do, but I was too tired. I lie down in the front bedroom and fell asleep. Suddenly, I was awakened by the sound of metal hitting the roof. I thought the Russians were near. As I looked down the road that came to my house, I saw someone coming, and I could feel myself going into shock from fear. I just knew it was a Russian coming. I felt my body trembling and could not talk. Then, I felt a hand beating on my back and a voice saying, "Edith, it's me, Martha!" My sister said it took her a few minutes to bring me back to my senses. She calmed me down, and later went to bed. We did not know what the next day would bring.

The next morning, Martha began packing some bags. Maybe she thought we would hook up the wagon and go to the hills. We fed our animals and then walked to town to a place where everyone gathered. A few men were burning German flags in front of the firehouse. I think everyone left in town gathered there to see what others were going to do.

A German soldier approached. He must have been a deserter. He was telling us he fought in Poland and saw what the Russians did to civilians. He said that in one little town in Poland, a bunch of young women were tied to a big table. They had been raped and their tongues and eyes had been cut out. When I heard that, it was more than I could handle. I ran back to the house and grabbed a couple of bags. I did not take the time to see what was inside the bags, whether there were any clothes for me. When I opened the bags later, I found only my sister's clothes.

I went back to town and saw some other girls, who were a little older than I, go up the hill to the main road where the German trucks were passing through with a lot of wounded soldiers. The girls thought the trucks might stop and pick us up. I decided to go with them. I turned around and yelled to my sister Martha, "Martha, please come with us," but she replied, "I have to stay here with grandmother and feed the animals." I was crying wondering if I was doing the right thing leaving her, but the sounds of the big guns were getting closer, and my fear was growing. I knew I had to run with the other girls to the German trucks.

The German soldiers stopped and loaded us onto the back of the trucks and then drove on. The soldiers told us they were trying to drive to Prague, because the Americans were already there, and nobody wanted to get captured by the Russians. The convoy drove slowly, and I learned that the trucks in the front had to check out the area and the little towns we drove through, because Czech partisans were attacking Germans and killing all they could. This became a nightmare for me, because we were Germans who had lived alongside the Czechs.

The first night, the wounded soldiers stopped in a wooded area. One soldier came to me and gave me a slice of brown bread with lots of butter and told me to be sure to eat it, since it might be a while before we got anything else to eat. He told me that when we got to the Americans and the war was over, he would take me home to his family and finish raising me. He felt sorry for me, because I was by myself with no family. At the time, it felt pretty good to hear that; it made me feel safe.

The next morning, we moved through a little town and passed some wagons loaded with belongings. The trucks stopped to see if they needed help, and that is when I saw my two brothers with my cousin Elsa. They begged me to take them with me, so the hardest thing was telling them that if I took them on the truck, they may be killed. I told them I felt they were safer with Cousin Elsa and that they would have food to eat. They both cried and it broke my heart.

We heard big guns from the distance, so it was time to hug my brothers with love and tears and say goodbye. Elsa told me that she witnessed women with their small children jump into a pond where they drowned, rather than get captured by the Russians. Elsa made a cross on my forehead and said, "God be with you." Soon, the trucks moved on, but we did not get very far. The partisans were shooting at the trucks. We had to lie down in the truck bed, and the soldiers covered us with something heavy, so the bullets would not hit us. We heard the bullets whistle by us, and I was so scared. As we drove slowly down the road, the attacks got worse. The soldiers said we would not make it to the Americans in time.

All of a sudden, the trucks stopped, and the soldiers told us civilians to run across the field and meet them on the other side. They were not sure if the trucks would make it through, because the gunfire was so heavy. As we ran, I passed a woman who was pushing a baby in a stroller. A bullet hit the baby, and I heard the woman scream, but I could not stop. We were all running for our lives. Finally, we made it across the field, and we waited for the trucks. Not everyone made it through the gunfire. We jumped back onto the trucks, and they rolled on.

Chapter 4
Running for My Life

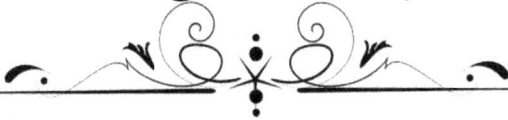

Towards evening, we could hear the big guns in the distance. I knew it was just a matter of time until we would meet our maker or get captured by the Russians. At dark, we arrived in Tabor and it looked like the entire town was in flames. All of the trucks stopped and we had to get out. Russian soldiers surrounded us and we put our hands up. They separated us civilians from the wounded German soldiers and that was the last time we saw them. I lost my friend who was going to take me home to his family. I clung to two girls, Anni and Gerti, from my hometown. They were a few years older than me. We had been away from home for two days, and our hope of getting to the Americans in Prague was now gone.

It took nearly all night for the Russians to decide what to do with us women and children. Finally, we were told we had to walk to the Austrian border, which was about 120 kilometers away. We had not had anything to eat or drink that day. The next day, we stayed close to all of the other refugees and began walking. We drank water from the river where everyone washed and God knows what else. We got our share of germs. Eventually, we saw a pump with a handle, and a lot of refugees were waiting for a turn to drink. As we got closer, we saw a Czech soldier hitting a man at the pump with the back part of a rifle, and we heard the man scream. No one could help him, or we would have gotten the same thing. The Czechs we had grown up with were no longer our friends, and I could not understand why they hated us so much.

When Anni, Gerti, and I got out of Tabor, we began searching for food. We had not eaten for three days, and I was getting weak because of my illness. I did not know how much longer I would last without food. As we went along in the countryside, we came across a big Bing cherry tree. It was like a miracle. We ate cherries until we were full, and I think that saved our lives.

That evening at dusk, we stopped in the woods for the night. As we lay on the ground, we heard horses coming our way, and we knew it would be Russians and Czechs looking for women to rape. We jumped up and ran deeper into the woods to hide. We had little sleep that night.

On the fourth day, we continued walking, looking for cherries to eat, and drinking water from a creek. That was how we survived for days, sleeping in the woods and always being on guard. Once in a while, the Czechs would give us a piece of brown bread, and when you are starving, that tastes so good.

One evening, we came to a small town and in a large field were a bunch of women and children in covered wagons. We had to find a place to hide for the night, and as we walked through the camp, two women spoke to us from their wagon. The back half was covered, and the front had a seat across it. The women were sitting on the seat holding their children. They told us we could crawl in the back and hide, and if the Russians should come, they would tell them there was only luggage in the back. They believed that the Russians would not hurt them, while they had small children on their laps. We got into the wagon. My left leg was already hurting from walking so much, but there wasn't enough room to lie down, so we had to sit up and not move. Soon, my leg began hurting so much that I tried to move. Anni and Gerti told me I had to sit still. If I moved, the cloth on the covered wagon would move and give us away.

We heard the Russian soldiers nearby, and I said a silent prayer. The soldiers walked up to the wagon, and the two women sitting up front with their children told the soldiers there was nothing but luggage behind the cover. As the Russians walked by, I felt a hand on my back, but the soldier went on to the next wagon. I knew then that God was watching over us. The Russian must have believed my back was part of the luggage. About ten minutes later, the same soldiers found some women, and we could hear the women screaming. That went on for quite a while… the voices and the screams.

Because of the severe pain in my leg, I began crying. I knew I had to get up soon and walk on that leg. We knew the soldiers were farther down in the field raping the girls and women, so we left the wagon and thanked the two women for saving us. We ran toward the woods and spent the rest of the night there. It was safer, plus we found other people there. Someone was always on the lookout. Our journey continued day by day. We walked during the day, slept in the woods at night, and drank dirty water from the creeks and rivers.

One evening, we walked by a Czech farmer who told us we could sleep in his barn, but we would have to leave by daybreak, so nobody could say he was hiding Germans. We were so grateful to him. His wife fixed us warm food, gave us lots of milk, and when we were leaving, she gave us bread for the road.

We were getting close to the border. I had a backpack with some clothes in it, but we had been told that the Czechs were taking everything away from the refugees, so we put on all the clothes we could wear. We crossed the border at Rets, Czechoslovakia, into Znaim, Austria. The border guards took everything we were carrying, but they did give us some bread. It wasn't enough to staunch my hunger, and I was getting weaker and weaker, so Anni gave me part of her bread.

Once we were in Austria, we felt safer and we walked along the railroad tracks toward Wien. We came alongside a parked train that was going to Wien, and the railroad workers let us catch a ride; it felt good to get off our feet for a while. In Wien, we were still in the Russian Zone, so we had to watch out and hide. The train stopped at the East Bahnhof train station in Vienna. Someone gave us food, and during the day, we were fairly safe from the Russians. At night, we slept in a little room on the floor of the station. One night, we heard Russians coming. They were drunk and loud. We hid under the window, so if they looked inside, they would not be able to see us. We spent three days and three nights at that station.

After the war was finally over, Anni and Gerti wanted to go back home. We walked from one little town to the next, begging for food along the way; a piece of bread now and then kept us going. I was getting weaker every day, and I did not know how much longer I would be able to keep going. It took a lot of effort to keep up with the girls, but my guardian angel was always beside me telling me, "You can do it!"

Three days after leaving Vienna, we walked into a small town where there was something like a soup kitchen to feed all the refugees coming through. They gave us Hungarian Goulash with bread. We found out later that it was made with horsemeat, but when you are starving, anything tastes good, and it gave us strength to continue toward the border.

We slept in the woods again, and when if we found a creek or a river, we splashed water on our faces. The fourth day started out like all of the others, walking in the hot sun. We had no food that day, but we found a fountain and got a drink of water. In the evening, we came to a town and asked some men for directions to the next town. We also met a lady and her daughter who lived in the next town, and we walked with them.

Out of town about a mile, we looked back and saw a large vehicle with a big spotlight coming toward us. The Russians would drive a little way, stop, and then turn the spotlight from left to right; it was as bright as daylight. We realized that the men we had asked directions from had told the Russian soldiers that five women were walking on the highway. We began running, but I did not have any strength left. Anni and Gerti each took one of my hands and pulled me, but I was slowing them down. When we came to a little hill, we thought we could hide behind it, and the Russians would not be able to see us from the highway. The area on the other side of the hill smelled like it was filled with dead horses. The odor was so bad we had to hold our noses, while we continued to run. Seeing the truck with the spotlight as it came closer and closer, gave us strength to go on. Anni kept saying, "Edith, you have to try harder to run!"

The lady we walked with said her house was the second one as we came into town. After reaching the town, we went through the ally and climbed over her fence. As we landed in her backyard, we heard the truck stop in front of the house. But once again, God watched over us and saved us. We stayed at the lady's house that night, and she gave us food. The men who had turned us in were Austrians, and that was hard to take.

The next day, we walked along the railroad tracks and covered more distance that way. Another day passed, and we spent that night in the woods. We always felt safest in the woods. We eventually arrived in Bernhardstal, which was by the Czech border, and since the war was over, we thought we could go back home. At the border, the Czech soldiers with rifles told us we could not come across the border. The mean look they gave us was enough for us to turn around and go back to Bernhardstal to find shelter.

In Bernhardstal, we began knocking on doors. At the first three or four houses, we were told they could not take us, because they already had refugees. When we came to a farm, an older lady said she could use some help. She had one room where all three of us could sleep. She was a widow with one son who worked on the farm. We did not have baggage to unpack, since we only had the clothes on our bodies, and we were hungry and thirsty. We asked if we could have something to eat, but she said we had to go out to the field and work to earn our food.

The day was very hot, and I was very weak. I knew I could not last much longer, but we went to the field and did what we were told. We were given water to drink, but that was not enough for me. After a couple of hours, I collapsed in the field. The farmer rushed us back to the house and gave us food.

In the evening, the old lady put a washtub in our room and heated water, so we could take a bath. It felt so good to sit in that tub of water and wash off all the dirt and sweat. We really felt relaxed. After I collapsed in the field, I think the farm lady realized we needed the rest. She let us go to sleep early that day. For the first time in almost a month, we slept in a bed and felt safe.

Chapter 5
Working to Live

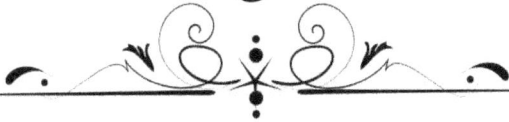

For the next two weeks, we worked in the fields. They brought lunch out to us, and we worked until evening. After supper, there was plenty to do at the farmhouse, like feeding the animals and cleaning the kitchen. We were glad to do whatever we were told. It meant so much to us to have a roof over our heads and food to eat. We felt safe, and that was our pay.

Times were really hard in the big cities. There was no food in the stores, so people rode the trains out to the country to exchange their clothes for food. That is how we got more clothes to wear, and we were very grateful.

After two weeks, the farm lady told us that her daughter, who lived in the next town, also had a farm and needed someone to take care of her little boy. The daughter's husband had not returned from the war. The farm lady asked me if I would go help her daughter, since I was still a child and not well. I had never told her I had tuberculosis, but I am sure she could tell. She told me I would not have to work in the fields, since the daughter already had refugees for that. That sounded really good to me. The next day, the farm lady got out the horse and buggy and drove me to Rabensburg to meet my new family.

I liked Mrs. Robinson right away, and the first thing she did was get rid of my lice. My hair was halfway down to my shoulders, and my head was full of lice and eggs. She soaked my head with kerosene and wrapped it with a big towel. My scalp was burning, but I was glad someone took enough interest to help me. After many hours, she removed the towel and washed my hair thoroughly. Then, we went outside on the porch and with a fine-toothed comb; she combed my hair for hours, removing all of the dead lice and eggs.

Getting three meals a day felt good. Breakfast was always brown bread with butter and jam that Mrs. Robinson had made. At lunch, she cooked a large meal for all of the people who worked there. For supper, we usually had brown bread again, but with goose fat on it. She made syrup from the sugar beets she grew, and we used that to put in the milk. Despite being well cared for, I became homesick for Anni and Gerti, and I cried every day. Anni and Gerti were as close to me as family, and I missed them as much as I missed my home and family. Also, I did not know if my family was dead or alive.

One evening, I decided to walk back to Bernhardstal to see Anni and Gerti. I walked on the railroad tracks, and the moon was so bright that I could see where I was going. When I had gone halfway down the track, I heard a lot of noise and singing coming from a small building. It was filled with Russians who sounded very drunk. I didn't know what to do. With the moon so bright, I was sure if they looked out the widow, they would see me. I was desperate to visit Anni and Gerti, so I took a chance and ran by really fast and made it to the girls' farm. They got upset with me for taking such a chance, walking so far at night. We had a long talk and then went to bed. The next morning, the farm lady got the wagon and drove me back to Rabensburg. I realized I should not have run off and should be grateful someone cared for me. I knew I had to grow up, so I stopped crying. I was thirteen-years-old.

I worked on the farm for the rest of the summer. About five or six people worked in the fields and Mrs. Robinson cooked their lunch and put it in big bags, and every day, I walked out to the fields with the food. The fields were close by, so the walk was not bad, except for the summer heat.

During the summer of 1945, thousands of cattle were brought out of Czechoslovakia by Russian soldiers, who looked like Mongols... very scary and mean-looking. As the Russians drove the cattle past the house, we stood behind the curtain of a little window and watched. I guessed that all the cattle had been taken from German families to be taken to Russia.

The work I did during the winter months from 1945 to 1946 was not hard. I fed the animals, cleaned the stalls, and helped take care of the four-year-old. Late in the spring of 1946, I met a lady who was going to Zabre to visit some relatives. Zabre was only three miles from my hometown of Kl. Jestreb. I asked her if she would deliver a letter to my family, if they were still alive. When the lady returned, she told me my family was still alive. That was the good news. The bad news was that Martha had been attacked two weeks after the war had ended. She had been walking to Zabre to get bread when two Russians tried to rape her. She fought them, and they hit her on the head and face with the butts of their rifles. Her screams brought people from a field to help her, and the two men ran away. For a year afterward, Martha did not know anyone. My aunt took food to Martha every day.

Our house had a large closed-in porch, and that's where Martha's bed was placed. One day, the Russians set our house on fire. Martha saw the flames coming up the walls, and she began to scream. The fire brought her out of shock, and she ran from the house. The house had burned shortly before the lady visited my hometown. My dad was still being held in a war prison by the Czechs. After the war was supposedly over, the Czechs killed a lot of Germans throughout the country.

I was extremely homesick for my family, but I had to accept that I had to make it on my own. I thanked God for keeping us all alive, even though we were miles apart. At least my family knew I was alive, so that was one less worry for them and me.

One day in June of 1946, I received a letter from my dad. That was a happy day for me. He had just come home from the Czech prison camp. Out of three-hundred men in that prison, he was only one of thirty that survived. Dad had never joined the Nazi party, and that and his faith in God saved his life. It must have been awfully hard on him to come home half-starved only to find his home burned to the ground and all of the animals gone, taken by the Czechs. However, he counted his blessings, because his four children were still alive.

Dad sent me the address of my uncle Ludwic, who lived in Vienna. I had never met Uncle Ludwic, but I wrote him right away, and I soon heard from him. My uncle lived only two hours by train. I was thrilled that I had family in the new country where I lived. I did not have any money, but Mrs. Robinson paid for my train ticket and let me go see my uncle, aunt, and cousin, Helga. They made me feel at home, and I was able to take a bath for the first time in a nice bathroom with running water.

My aunt and uncle had a large apartment with nice furniture, including a piano, which Helga played for me. I wanted to play, also, so she taught me to read some notes. They have stayed with me over the years. My uncle insisted that I be confirmed at the Catholic Church, which usually occurs after first communion. I loved all the attention I got, but after two days, I had to return to Rabensburg. Within a month, my uncle had made all of the arrangements for my confirmation, and Mrs. Robinson gave me a few days off. My aunt bought me a light-blue dress and some new shoes. On the "big day," my uncle was my chaperone. First, we went by streetcar to St. Stefans Church, a well-known church in Vienna. Half of the church was bombed out, but what was left was beautiful. A bishop performed the ceremony and I received another middle name, Ludwika, after Uncle Ludwic, who was my sponsor.

When we left the church, a horse and buggy were waiting. My uncle, wanting to surprise me, had made the reservation. The buggy was decorated with flowers, and I felt like Cinderella. We rode around the city for a good hour, and then the whole family took me for dinner. That evening, we went to an opera. That was my big day, and when that day was over, I felt as if it had all been a dream. Nothing that nice had ever happened to me before.

The next day, I had to return to my job on the farm. I was 14 ½ years old. My uncle said I could stay with his family and work for him, but I did not feel right not going back to Mrs. Robinson and her little boy. She had been so good to me, taking me in, and she needed me on the farm, because her husband had still not returned from the war.

One day, Mrs. Robinson grabbed a shovel and began digging in the backyard. She had hidden some boxes containing her fine linen from the Russians, but when we opened the boxes, all of her things had been ruined by mildew. They had been in the ground too long. I really felt bad for her.

On another day, Mrs. Robinson took me to a photographer to have my picture taken. In the photograph, you can see the hard life I had lived, but I looked a lot better than I had a year earlier when the war ended. At that time, I was near death… weak from hunger and tuberculosis.

At the end of September of 1946, I received a letter from my dad who was in Germany. My family had been thrown out of Kl.

Jestreb and shipped to Germany. A farmer gave them one room in which to cook, sleep, and live… for four people… and Dad was grateful. At least I knew they were safe and away from the Russians and Czechs.

I was told that since I was a refugee in Austria, I could not get papers to go to Germany. I could not understand the law. I was still a child. Why couldn't I be reunited with my family? But, since my family only had one room to live in and hardly any food to eat, I would have been just another worry for my dad if I had joined them. I was still sick with tuberculosis, so I told myself I would be better off staying on the farm with Mrs. Robinson. At least I was getting enough to eat.

In the spring of 1947, Anni and Gerti decided to leave the farm. They found a job in Vienna and lived together in a boarding house for students. They told me about it and said the lady had a son who was a doctor and was engaged to a girl in Steyer, Austria, which was in the American Zone. The girl's father was also a doctor, and his family was looking for a maid. I could have that job. Although I didn't like to leave Mrs. Robinson, I caught the train to Vienna.

Chapter 6
My New Home

I arrived at my uncle's home in Vienna, and he took me to see Anni and Gerti, as well as to meet the young doctor, who explained how he was going to use his girlfriend's passport to take me across the Russian border into the American Zone. To get out of the Russian Zone sounded good, but I knew if I got caught, I could end up in Siberia. Still, I wanted badly to get out of the Russian Zone, and this was my chance.

Although the Austrians had begun to live normal lives again, two years after the war had ended; the farmers had more to eat than the people in Vienna. I knew if I did not take this chance to leave, I might never have another opportunity. When I told my uncle of my decision, he tried to talk me out of it, saying I could live with them and work in their business. He said I should stay with my relatives, rather than with strangers, but a little voice inside told me to go ahead with my plans, so I went back to the farm.

Telling Mrs. Robinson I wanted to leave was hard. She had become like a mother to me. When it was time to go, she gave me a suitcase that was made from straw and a coat that she had bought earlier for me; it was a light coat made from burlap and went well with my straw suitcase. When I left, I promised I would write. Mr. Robinson was still a war prisoner in France, but it looked like he would be home soon.

When I arrived in Vienna, my uncle drove me to the home where Anni and Gerti worked. I thanked him for everything, and he again tried to talk me into coming to his house. He finally realized that my mind was made up. After I had a short visit with Anni and Gerti, the doctor put my suitcase in the car, along with his. It was hard telling Anni and Gerti goodbye, not knowing when I would see them again.

As we drove off, the doctor told me that when we reached the Russian border in Enns, that I should put on a scarf and hold on to the two suitcases and stay bent over, so the Russians could not see my face. He said the border patrol knew him fairly well, because he traveled back and forth often with his girlfriend. He was pretty sure they would not check us too closely. As we got closer to the border, my stomach began to hurt, and my legs became like rubber. Thoughts ran through my mind that if I got caught by the Russians, it would be the end for me. I could not let the fear I felt show in my face, so I began praying. I knew God was with me and would protect me, like He had done over the years. He had saved me from danger and illness, and that thought gave me the strength to get out of the car, holding on to the suitcases. The doctor handed the passports to the Russians, and I heard them say, "Yes, yes; it is okay. You can go." I understood that much Russian. We got back to his car and drove across the bridge toward the American Zone border. I was not afraid at all facing the other side. All the fear I had was gone, as the Americans smiled and waved us on. My guardian angel had protected me again.

We drove another hour from Enns to Steyer, which looked big to a girl who had always lived on a farm in the country. We drove up to a large, fancy villa, and I read the name *Dr. Rodolf Pesl*. The young doctor drove through the gate to the back of the house. I got my raggedy suitcase, went into the house, and met my new family. I felt like a *nobody* around educated people, but they were friendly toward me. They fixed the young doctor and me something to eat.

The young doctor was happy to see his fiancée, Waltraud, who was the oldest daughter of the five children of my new family. Their grandmother, Mrs. Pesl, also lived there. Dr. Pesl was still in an American war prison, but was expected to be released soon. I thought to myself that there had to have been a good reason for Americans to hold a prisoner for two years. About the only Germans held that long were SS, and before they were released, they had to be cleared of all crimes. After I was with the family for two weeks, the doctor came home from prison. The family was happy to have him home, and nothing was said in front of me, and I did not ask any questions.

It took the doctor about two weeks to get strong enough to open his medical practice again and to call all of his old patients to see if they wanted him to be their doctor again. He was well-liked as a doctor, so he had no trouble rebuilding his practice.

For a fifteen-year-old, I had plenty to do. I cleaned eight rooms, helped in the kitchen, and every Monday, I washed clothes for eight people, as well as the things for the practice. I washed everything by hand on a scrub board and had a brush for tough stains. I would build a fire under a big kettle and fill it with water and soap powder. I would boil all the sheets and whites, rinsing everything in a huge cement tub, and then I would hang everything outside. At the end of the work day, I would really be tired, but I never told them I had tuberculosis. I felt like I was slowly getting stronger.

Two families lived upstairs in that big villa. Perhaps, Mrs. Pesl had to take them in after the war to get the rent money to feed the family, since the doctor was still in prison. I never had a room there. I slept in a curtained-off bed in a hallway, and one family used that hallway to get to their apartment, so the only time I spent there was when I went to bed.

On the farm, I never received wages, but I had food and a roof over my head, plus used clothing. I felt pretty fortunate in hard times. I worked long days, but at least it was not dust and sweat like at the farm, and I did not mind all the work. Just knowing I was free from the Russians was worth more to me than riches.

Once in a while, the doctor and his wife would take me with them when they went out to the country to make house calls. The country people paid the doctor with fresh vegetables and meat. One day, the doctor had to take some blood from a rather stout lady patient. He asked me to hold a bowl, and he made an incision in the woman's arm. The blood squirted out into the bowl. Seeing all of that blood caused me to feel odd. I had just enough time to hand the doctor the bowl and leave the room before I was sick to my stomach. The doctor later told me that I would never make a nurse.

One family that lived in the villa had a daughter, Gertrand, and she and I became friends. She was a year older than me. In the evenings after work, I usually went to her apartment for a little while. I learned to play a few games, and her parents included me in their family times together. My sixteenth birthday came and went just like any other day. One weekend Gertrand said, "Let's go dancing." I told her I had never been on a dance floor, and she assured me that was no problem. Her family gave me a dress to wear, and I had one pair of fairly decent shoes. Off we went. The dancehall, which was within walking distance from our house, was nice, and I was already watching how the couples were making their steps. Gertrand knew boys from school there, and she told them I wanted to learn to dance. To my surprise, I learned really fast how to tango and waltz.

After that first time, Gertrand and I went dancing every Saturday evening, and in about three to four weeks, I felt like a pro on the dance floor. Dancing also gave me something to look forward to on the weekends. However, I was still very bashful and felt like an orphan among the other girls. They all had nice clothes to wear, but I got used to that. One thing for sure, I never had to sit and watch others dance. Boys always came and asked me to dance. I was really light on my feet.

One day, I thought I would like to learn to ice skate. I rented a pair of skates and shoes, and the music sounded so nice. I felt pretty brave and figured that if others could do it, so could I. Holding on at first made it easier, then I was all by myself slowly skating along. That was a great afternoon, but I never returned, although I would have loved to. I could not afford the fee.

Months went by, and the workload never changed. The doctor's family kept me busy all day. In the evenings, I visited with Gertrand, and sometimes, we would walk to town and look in the store windows. I enjoyed looking at the pretty dresses, but never had the money to buy one. The doctor's oldest daughter gave me some used clothing once in a while, which made me very happy. To me, it was like getting something new to wear.

Soon after my seventeenth birthday, I decided to find a job that paid more. I found one in a bakery. They were looking for a cook, and although I told them I had never cooked before, I got the job. I had learned by watching food being prepared at the doctor's house. I also bought a big cookbook called *Wiener Kitchen*. I only made five schillings more on that job, but I had a private room, and I did not have to clean house. I was pretty brave. I had to cook for eight people, but by using the cookbook, I learned to cook and the people liked what I fixed. Soon, they let me plan meals. I enjoyed pleasing them.

After eight months there, in early 1950, I heard about a job with an American family who was looking for a maid. When I saw how much more they paid, I applied and got the job. From one-hundred twenty-five schillings a month, I went to three-hundred, more than double what I earned at the bakery. Both the American man and woman spoke German. He was with the Civilian Investigation Center (CIC) and wore civilian clothes on his job. I could tell they were important people.

During the summer of 1950, the family planned to drive to Germany for vacation, so they said they would take me with them across the border to visit my family. I was real excited to see my family after five years. I packed my little straw suitcase and off we went. We drove for about two hours to the Austrian border. My boss got out and showed them their visa, then pointed at me and told the guards I worked for them, but I did not have papers, but they wanted to take me to Germany to see my family. I was told I could not cross the border without papers and even though my boss tried to talk to the border police, it was useless. I decided I would cross the border illegally by going over the mountain. My boss thought it was too risky. I asked him if he would take my suitcase into Germany to my relatives' house, which was right across the border and tell them I was coming over the mountain. My boss turned the car around, drove far enough back, until we were out of the border guards' sight, and dropped me off.

I ran into the woods deep enough so no one could see me from the highway. After walking for about fifteen minutes, I reached the steep of the hill I had to go over. To my dismay, I saw that it was a bare hill with no trees; I was in open view of the border guards below. About halfway up the hill, I heard the border patrol's dogs barking. I just knew they must have seen me. I crawled faster up the hill, but I slipped down until I was able to grab a branch and hold on to keep from slipping farther down. Since my dress had short sleeves, my arms were scratched and bloody, but I did not have time to worry about that. I was so afraid that the border guards had seen me and were coming after me that I got up and started up that hill again. The second time, I made it to the top. Below, I saw fields of green grass and a road going toward the little town where my relatives lived. I finally felt safe.

I wasn't far from my relatives' house, and I soon saw my cousin, Franz, standing by a tower waiting for me. The doctor had found my relatives and dropped my little suitcase off. I was so happy to see Franz. He thought it would be best if he walked with me through the town to his house, because the border guards lived in town, and if they saw me walking by myself, they might get suspicious, especially since my arms were bloody.

My aunt cleaned me up, washed the blood off my arms, and put medicine on my cuts. My relatives and I enjoyed each others' company, and we had a lot to talk about. They wanted to know all about my escape and the five years since I had left Czechoslovakia. I told them some of the horrible things I went through and my close calls with death. My aunt made a cross on my forehead with holy water and said to me, "You are a walking miracle my child." My Grandmother Schubert, who was also staying with my aunt, was very ill, and they did not expect her to live much longer.

Since I only had two weeks in Germany, I was eager to catch the train and go see Dad, Martha, Burkhard, and Helmut. Franz

My Journey to Freedom, the Edith Schubert Story

went on the bus with me to Berchtesgaden, where I caught the train. It was a good feeling having someone looking out for me, but once on the train, I was on my own again. In the early afternoon, the train stopped at the Munich station. I was shocked at what I saw. Most of the station was bombed out and the people looked poor. They wore raggedy clothes like mine, so I did not feel too out of place. At the station, I caught a train to Augsburg. In Augsburg, I caught another train that took me out to a small town from where I walked to the farmhouse where Dad, Burkhard, and Helmut lived. My dad's house had one large room in which they cooked and slept. Still, it was a happy reunion. After resting for two days at my dad's, visiting my aunt and uncle and my Grandpa and Grandma Kretchi, I was ready to undertake the long trip to see Martha, who lived some distance away. Burkhard and Helmut had bicycles, so Burkhard said he would take the trip with me, and I could ride Helmut's bike. But, Helmut became upset because he wanted to go with us. I hated to leave him behind, because we had not seen each other in five years. His crying really upset me.

Riding through a big city like Augsburg was no picnic. One of our aunts lived a couple of hours from Augsburg, so we went there first to rest and get something to eat. I had not ridden a bicycle in more than five years, so my bottom was really sore; I could hardly walk. Our aunt was really happy to see us. Her home-cooked meal was so good, and it gave us the strength to ride another two hours to see Martha. On the way out the door, our aunt said to us, "Go with God," and she made a cross on our foreheads with holy water. She had been my favorite aunt when we lived in Czechoslovakia. I often walked alone to her house, just to get a good meal. I walked

45

through the woods and wasn't afraid. I guess I had lots of courage as a child with my guardian angel by my side.

Our ride to Martha's place took us through little country towns, until we reached the farm where she and her husband worked. It was great seeing my sister again. Her face still showed marks from her injuries caused by the Russians who had attacked and tried to rape her. I met her husband, and right away, I did not like him. He treated my sister like she was a slave. She did everything just to keep peace. They both had plenty to do, milking many cows in the morning and evening.

Burkhard and I stayed two days at the farm, so we had plenty of milk to drink. Martha was raising a little fawn. We fed it with a bottle, which I enjoyed so much. The fawn followed us wherever we walked, just like a puppy. Those two days went by too fast. I realized how much I missed my homeland, the farm we had, the animals, and my family.

When it was time for us to leave, Burkhard and I said goodbye and rode our bicycles the three hours back to Dad's place, where I spent another week. While Dad was working, I would walk to the next town to visit relatives. One day, Grandpa Kretchi took me by train to Augsburg. He wanted to treat me that day, so we had lunch and then he bought me some nice material for a dress. I was really happy with that since I hardly had anything to wear and what I did have was all hand-me-downs.

Cousin Helga, who was only six days older than I, had just had a baby. Back home, she had always had everything. My aunt and uncle spoiled her. She was eighteen-years-old, but they still took care of her and the baby. How different our lives were. I knew nothing but hardship and sorrow; Helga had nothing but love and protection. All she talked about was herself, and she gave me the feeling she thought she was better than everyone else. I did not tell her much about my last five years, how I had to struggle to survive. Still, I held my head up; at least I was supporting myself.

The day came for me to return to Schellenberg. When I arrived, I was told they had buried by Grandmother Schubert, so I had missed the funeral. Franz helped me plan how to cross the border back into Austria. By showing my grandmother's funeral notice, I could tell the border guards that I had come across the border for the funeral. I would not have to climb the mountain. Franz had a little wagon, so we went through the woods pretending to gather wood. We passed a couple of sheds and felt that border guards were hiding in there, but we kept going toward the border. When Franz thought I was safe, we said goodbye. One of the guards in the shed saw Franz returning alone, so he phoned the Austrian border patrol, and in a matter of minutes, I was picked up and taken to the Austrian border. They read me the riot act, and I was so scared. I had broken the law when I crossed the border, and even when I showed them my grandmother's funeral notice as the reason I crossed the border, that did not help. They gave me a choice: pay twenty schillings or spend three days in jail. I had just enough money to pay the fine and still be able to buy a train ticket back to Steyer. I was completely stressed out by the time I returned to work.

Toward the end of 1950, we learned that Steyer would be closed down, and all of the Americans would either be transferred or sent back to the United States. I had heard that the United States was taking refugees through a Catholic organization, so I thought that by immigrating, I would have a chance to better my life. I put my papers in, and I was accepted. However, because I was only eighteen, I had to get my dad's permission. I wrote to him right away and told him of my plans. He refused to sign, saying I was too young to move to a strange land. I got upset with him and wrote back that he had no right to hold me back; I had been on my own since I was thirteen, and I had to survive without the family. The immigration people already had a job as a maid for me in New York, but by the time my dad finally gave me permission to leave, it was too late. The United States had stopped all immigration. I was really upset, but I guess it was not meant to be. I believe everything happens for a reason.

Chapter 7

Joe

Here I was again, looking for another job, but I did not want to work for Germans anymore. They hardly paid anything. So, my boss lady drove me to the employment office in Linz, and I found a job as a maid in Horsching with another American family. We returned to Steyer, and I packed my little suitcase. My boss lady gave me a few dresses, and I was so happy. The next morning, I went by bus to Horsching, and the bus even stopped for me in front of the American housing area. I found my new family. The wages were the same, plus room and board.

In the spring of 1951, that family transferred back to the States, so I found another family to work for. They didn't have an extra room, so I had to take a room in Horsching with a German family. Almost everything I made went to pay for that room, but Frau Wanke became like a mother to me. Every day when I came home from work, she had a bowl of soup or something for me to eat. It seemed like I was always hungry. Later, I met an older lady who was a friend of Frau Wanke's who lived down the road from us, and she also fixed meals for me.

A lot of refugees were in Horsching, so I did not feel out of place in that little town. The Austrian government had built a camp outside of town for refugees, and one building was for entertainment. Dances were held there on Saturdays. The band was made up of refugees. I enjoyed going there and hearing the music from back home. My thoughts would wander, and I would remember what I had lost.

Going and coming from work, I always walked by the house of a girl named Doti. One day, she asked if I was interested in meeting an American soldier who was new on post and worked for her boyfriend. Although I was very bashful and spoke little English, I agreed to meet him. One afternoon, Doti and I walked to where he lived and worked. When I met Joe, he was bashful too. We made a lot of eye contact, but he was not much of a talker, and half of what he said to me, I did not understand. Joe wanted to see me again, and I felt the same way, but I knew I had to learn to speak English better, so he and I could talk to each other.

On our second date, Joe and I felt more at ease with each other, and after that, we saw one another more often. The transmitter site where Joe worked was located outside the Army base not far from where I worked. Sometimes, I visited him, which was okay with his boss. Joe always had something for me to eat. I was always hungry. Rice Krispies was my favorite cereal. One day, Joe had a whole half-gallon of vanilla ice cream for me, and I ate the entire half-gallon by myself. Needless to say, I did not crave ice cream for a long time.

Joe came to see me when he was off duty. Frau Wanke really liked him, so I think he felt at home. She was like a mother to me, and because I had been separated from my family at age thirteen, I was starving for love and affection. Months went by, and I knew that Joe's tour of duty would soon be over, and I could not see myself staying in Horsching working as a maid and making very little money. I had met a girl named Eva, also a refugee, who worked in the same housing area as I did, and we became good friends. Eva and I walked to Horsching every evening. One day, Eva and I decided to put our immigration papers in for Canada. Shortly after that, Eva met a young man from Hungary, also a refugee, and began to date him. She still said she would go to Canada with me. One day, Joe came to see me and told me he was being transferred to Tullin Air Base outside of Vienna, but he promised to stay in touch, and he did. Once a month, he came down on a special train to see me. He also wrote me letters, so that helped when I was lonely.

Months went by, and Eva and I did not hear anything from the Canadian immigration office. Then, in early 1953, Eva told me she was pregnant and could not immigrate with me. At first I was scared, but later, I decided to stay strong and face what came. Two weeks later, I received a date for my physical. I became worried about the tuberculosis I had, not knowing if I was healed. Prayer always helped, and I knew God was watching over me and had saved me from harm and danger over the years, so it was really up to Him.

One day, while I was still waiting for the results of my physical, I received a letter from Joe saying that he was being sent back to Horsching for the last four or five months of his tour. It was good news to have him close again, but I was sad knowing we had to say goodbye for good in July. I decided to just take one day at a time.

The letter finally came from the immigration office that said my travel was approved. The next day, I caught the bus to Linz to get my papers. There I was told that my x-rays showed two scars on my lungs, but I was healed from the tuberculosis. How many people do you see who have tuberculosis, walked for an entire month with hardly anything to eat, worked doing hard labor, and still survive tuberculosis? Nothing but God!

The date for my departure for Canada was in November of 1953, and as of that date, I belonged to the Canadian government. With my new papers, I could meet my family at the German border. I wrote my dad right away, so everyone could make plans, and Joe was coming with me, so they could all meet him. When I told Eva I had all my papers for Canada, she became sad, because she did not want me to move away.

The thought of traveling to Canada alone really scared me, but I told myself that I was a survivor, and I could handle the challenge. Frau Wanke was happy for me to start a new life, but sad that I was moving away; she loved me like her own daughter.

The spring of 1953 came and went fast. I was busy with my job and planning for my future, and then one day, when I was visiting

Joe at work, out of the blue, he asked me to marry him. Of course I said yes, but at the same time, I knew there wouldn't be a wedding before he went back to the States. In June, Joe and I traveled to the German border where we attended a family get-together in a restaurant. My dad came with Martha and her little son Werner, and my brothers came on a motorbike. My Grandfather Kretchi and some relatives were also there. Everybody liked Joe right away, except for my grandfather. His reason was that I was leaving the country for Joe.

Joe and I had about a month left together, and it went much too fast. He bought me two suitcases, since I never had any extra money. The day he left for Bremerhaven, I met him at the transmitter site to say goodbye. That was one of the hardest things I ever had to do. I cried the rest of the day. Since I barely made enough money to live on, Joe promised he would send me ten dollars a month toward the train ticket I needed to get to Bremerhaven.

Eva was getting married during the first part of August. She was already six months pregnant. Neither of us had the money to buy a dress, so we went on the bus to the city to a rental place. Eva found a nice white dress, and I got a long gray dress. The wedding, which was like an Italian wedding, went well with lots of food, music, and dancing. Eva's in-laws paid for everything and showered her with much love. When I saw that she was taken care of, it made my departure easier.

The last three months were pretty hectic. Letters from Joe came often, and I received the first ten dollars in August. Still, I had lots of worries. How would I get to the big train station in Linz? I also found out I had to see the Catholic priest to sign some papers, so I could leave Austria without owing any money. To my surprise, the priest informed me that I never paid any church taxes, while living in Horsching. He said I made eight-hundred schillings a month like a secretary, but I only made three-hundred schillings a month as a maid. I had to prove to him I only made three-hundred schillings, which was barely enough to live on, so then I was excused from paying church taxes, and he signed my papers.

In September, Joe sent another ten dollars, but when I figured out my expenses, I realized I would have to have thirty dollars more in October. Then, a strange thing happened. I dreamed clearly how I walked up to the window at the post office. They handed me my mail, and there was a letter from Joe. I said, "Dear God, I need thirty dollars." I opened the letter, and sure enough, it contained thirty dollars! And that was exactly how it happened the next morning when I went to the post office. They handed me Joe's letter, and he had sent thirty dollars. The American family I worked for changed the dollars for schillings.

I was almost ready to leave, but saying goodbye to Frau Wanke was so hard to do. Frau Schulze and her friend brought me to Linz and helped me get on the train for Bremerhaven. Goodbyes are always hard, and I left with a heavy heart, not knowing what lay ahead.

On the train, I met a girl named Paula, who was from Linz. She was also immigrating to Canada, so we had a lot to talk about, which helped pass the time. It was a long ride, and we were tired when we arrived in Bremerhaven. From there, we rode the bus to a barracks where we stayed two days before we got on the boat. A lot of people were staying in the barracks, and about half of them were immigrating to Australia.

Chapter 8

Canada, My Journey to Freedom

When our ship, the *Arosa Kulm* pulled away from the harbor in Bremerhaven, I began crying, wondering if I had done the right thing. I had already lost my homeland, and now, I was giving up my country, not knowing if I would ever see my family again. I think I cried for two days. Our ship had to make a stop in London to pick up more people, but when we got to the English Channel, the ship had to wait for two days because of heavy fog. In London, more people came on board our small ship. A total of five hundred people were sailing for Canada. While our ship was docked in London, we had a good view of Big Ben.

The room we slept in held twenty-three people. We slept on cots; Paula was at the bottom, and I was on top. As soon as we left London, Paula got seasick. I was trying hard not to. Joe had told me to eat three meals a day, so I wouldn't get sick and that worked for six days. On the seventh day, after returning from the dining room and starting down the stairs to the room, I saw a woman throwing up in a bucket, and that caused me to get sick, as well. After that, for the next six days, every meal I ate came right back up. We were in the middle of the ocean, and in November, the sea is pretty rough, which didn't help matters.

Paula was getting really weak and hardly left her bed. I was a little braver and went on deck when the waves weren't too big. Our boat was overloaded with people, so it was a miracle we even made it to Canada alive. On the twelfth day, we entered the Canadian canal on the St. Lawrence River, and the boat stopped rocking; my sea sickness stopped also. That was a wonderful feeling.

After two days in the canal, we landed in Quebec. Getting off the ship took a while, and I became scared because almost all of the people were speaking French. I kept looking for Joe. I thought he would surprise me and be there, but that was wishful thinking. I knew he couldn't come that far. It was half a day before everyone was off the ship and had collected their luggage. The large waiting room had heat, and we saw T.V. screens on the walls. That was my first time to see a T.V., and even though it was in French, it was interesting to watch.

Paula was weak from not eating for twelve days, so we stayed close to each other. By evening, the buses came and took us to a camp for one night. We got a hot meal, and I was ready for bed. The next morning, we got on the bus and headed for Montreal, where we spent another night in another camp. The next day, after breakfast, we received our final instructions for the two-day train ride to Winnipeg. We were also given the names of the families we would be working for. Around noon, we were taken to the train station, and before we boarded, we received big name tags, which we pinned to our clothes, and then off we went. After the train pulled out of Montreal, we saw a lot of bare land and swamp areas. I wondered where we would end up, but overall, it wasn't too bad. We were fed well, and the sleeper was comfortable.

Two days later, we arrived in Winnipeg, and we were taken by taxi to the address we had been given. I was extremely tired when I got to where I was to work. The family was Jewish. When I walked into the house, the woman never asked me how my trip was or if I was hungry. The first thing she said was, "We pay you sixty dollars a month and not more, no matter who much work you do." I had my own thought on that remark, but I was glad to have a place to stay and food to eat.

There were two sweet little girls in the family, and we became pretty close. When I wasn't cleaning the house, I played with them, and that's all I had to do there. The woman did all of the cooking. I had one year to pay back the Canadian government for the trip, which came to $160, so I decided to repay it in four months, paying back $40 month. I made do with the remaining $20.

Joe was stationed at Scott Air Force Base in Illinois, so I sent him my new address. A week later, I was watching for the mailman. When I did hear from him, he told me he would come up for Christmas. I got really excited, and that helped me from getting too homesick. My room was in the basement, but I had no privacy since it was an open area. All I had was a bed and a dresser with a coffee table and one chair, but I did have a private bathroom. In Austria, Joe had given me a radio, and I had brought it with me, so in the evenings, I listened to music and wrote letters to Joe or my family in Europe.

Christmas Eve arrived, and I was wondering if Joe would make it. The weather was cold, and snow was on the ground. That evening, the doorbell rang. I opened the door, and there he was... cold, tired, and hungry. I was so happy to see him. I asked the woman for the night off, and then Joe and I drove around some and parked and talked. He said he had to sleep in the car while visiting me, because he had no extra money for a motel. I didn't have any money to give him, since I wouldn't get paid until the end of the month. I felt very sorry for him, because the nights were so cold. The next day, with what money he had, Joe went to a garage to get a bigger thermostat installed, so the car would be warmer. Joe was able to stay two more days in Winnipeg, but each day, I had to work till afternoon. Then, Joe would pick me up, and we would spend the evenings together. The time to say goodbye came again. Joe had to return to Scott Air Force Base to attend school for six months, so I knew I wouldn't see him until then; it was a tearful goodbye.

In January, Paula and I signed up for night school to better our English. We had to walk about six blocks to school, and the weather was terribly cold. A few times, it reached 40 below, and by the time I got home, my legs would be red all the way up. I wore a warm scarf around my head and my mouth. Breathing into the scarf caused icicles to form. That part was no fun, but in the long run, it paid off, since my English improved a lot. I also sent my first $40 to the government, and the $20 I had left just covered what I had to have. But weeks went by, and I didn't hear from Joe. At first I thought the school was keeping him busy, but after a while, I thought that wasn't reason enough not to find time to write. Finally, in February, I received a letter from him, and then nothing again until April. Those two months were really bad for me, watching for the mailman every day and then nothing. I couldn't concentrate on my work, and I felt depressed. All I could do was wait and cry.

I paid off my loan in April and finished night school, so I felt good about that. The letter from Joe that I had received in April didn't tell me much. One of the reasons he had given me for not writing was that he had to concentrate on his school work. Early in May, I received another letter from him. He said that as soon as his school was out in July, he would get ten days leave and would come to Winnipeg, so we could get married. My heart filled with joy, and I told my boss lady right away. She said, "It's good to see you smile again."

I saved all of the money I could to buy a wedding dress and a pair of shoes. The dress wasn't anything fancy. I had to get by with what I had. I also began looking for a room to rent in July. I was counting the days. I had about $100 saved, and that paid for a few things. When Joe arrived, he only had $20 in his pocket, so that changed a few things. I had to cancel the reservation at a little restaurant for the evening meal after the wedding.

We went to a Catholic church to see if they would marry us, but the bishop informed us that Joe would have to learn the 21 questions and live in Canada for two weeks. Joe was willing to learn the 21 questions, but he only had ten days leave. We finally went to a Baptist church and made an appointment for July 9th. Next, we had to get a blood test. Paula's boss was a doctor, so we went to him, and I had mine taken first. The area where the needle had gone in immediately swelled up to the size of an egg. I showed my arm to Joe before he went in to have his blood drawn. Joe's face had turned white, and his lips were blue. He told me to stay calm, but I had never seen anyone pass out before, so I got out of the car and ran to the doctor's office for help. They knew right away what had happened. A nurse held something under Joe's nose, and he opened his eyes. What brought all that on was when he saw my arm; he said he couldn't stand to see me hurt.

On July 8th, we went to the courthouse and got married there. The next day, we had a short ceremony in the office of the Baptist church. Joe had brought a friend of his from the States, and he and one of my girlfriends acted as our witnesses. I really missed my family and wished they could have been there to share my joy, especially my dad. He was one in a million and had a heart of gold.

After the ceremony, we went to a studio for a few pictures and then we went to supper... the four of us. That's all we could afford. For the rest of the time we had together, we ate soup and sandwiches, and I had to borrow some money from my boss. Our families couldn't help us, so we did the best we could. We spent the next few days in the room or at the grocery store. We had two hot plates, so we were able to heat the soup. Joe's friend had a room in the same building, but he spent most of the day with us. He gave us a nice hand-painted tea set for a wedding gift, and that was the only gift we received. Joe's mom wrote me and told me she would give me a wedding shower when I came to the States, but that never happened.

The day came to say goodbye. Tears always went with goodbyes. I returned to work. After eating soup and sandwiches for ten days, I was ready for home-cooked meals. My boss lady was a good cook, but she never fixed anything from pork, because Jews don't believe in eating pork. I had a lot to do to get the paperwork together to go to the States. I had to put in for a visa, which I was told would take three months. I also had to take a physical, and I knew what they would find. Thank God I was healed or I would still be in Austria.

Joe had been transferred to Edwards Air Force Base in California, so his family was to meet me in Pueblo, Colorado to take me to their home in Penrose. I slowly prepared myself for the next long journey. I went shopping a few times to buy a few gifts for Joe's family. The three months went by pretty fast; Joe's letters kept me strong. They were like food for the body. It is hard to imagine what it was like trying to do everything by myself. I needed my family so much for guidance and love, but looking back, I can see that God was always by my side, giving me the strength to go on.

My visa was ready in the middle of October. I wasted no time getting my train ticket. I had my last get-together with Paula and Betty. The family I worked for hated to see me go, and I dearly loved the two little girls. I called a taxi to take me to the train station. I had a big overseas trunk and one suitcase that Joe had bought for me in Austria, so I needed help loading and unloading on the train. The train was an evening train leaving for St. Paul, Minnesota, and for the rest of the night, I had a sleeper. The train took all night to get to St. Paul, and then I had an 8-hour wait for the next train to Colorado. I called a girl I knew who lived in St. Paul. She was originally from Berlin, and we had met in Winnipeg. She stayed with me until I got on the train again.

I couldn't get a sleeper for the second night, so it was a long night of sitting up, but early the next morning, we arrived in La Junta. The train stopped there to let people on, mostly Mexicans and Indians. I became pretty scared, not knowing what kind of people they were. They looked very poor. Soon, my fear left me, and I felt sorry for them. I knew what it feels like to be poor. A few hours later, I reached Pueblo where Joe's parents met me. When the train stopped, I was so nervous that my heart was beating wildly. I was greeted by my in-laws and Joe's sister, Freda. The first twenty-three years of my life were over; a new life had begun, but I will never forget my childhood years and *my journey to freedom*.

About the Author

Though my childhood and young adulthood years were hard, and not receiving much of an education, I feel I accomplished a lot in my life. My husband Joe was my "hero" and provided lots of love and support. I went to school in 1960 for American History, so I could pass the test for American Citizenship. My greatest accomplishment was receiving that certificate and writing the memoir of my life. My strength came from God and without Him; I wouldn't be here today to tell my story.

I'm on the far left on the
Arosa Kulm ship immigrating
to Canada. (November 1953).

I am twelve-years-old, ▶
one year before the
war ended.

On the farm in
Rabensburg, 1946.
▼

◀ *Our little Catholic church in my hometown, holding many memories.*

My Aunt Hilda's wedding in 1938. I'm standing at the far left next to my Grandma.
▼

▲

We were acting silly on the ship the Arosa Kulm excited about reaching Canada soon.

The two little girls in Canada where I worked as a maid in 1954. ▼

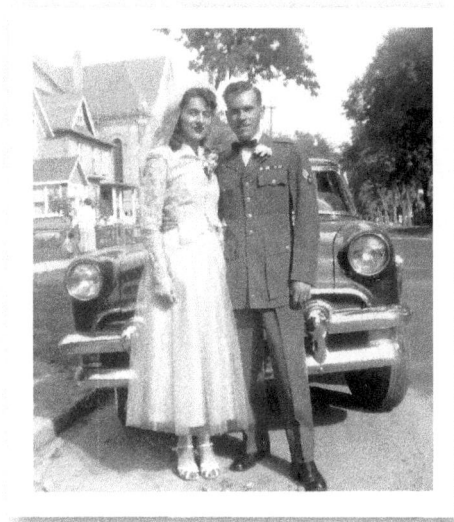

Our wedding on July 9, 1954.

My Uncle Alois' wedding in 1944.
He never returned home from the war.

◀ *Edith Schubert Combs,*
fourteen-years-old,
1946 in Rabensburg,
Austria, occupied by Russia.

My parents' wedding, ▶
February 6, 1923.

◄ Edith in 1948 with a friend in Steyer, Austria, age 16.

Combs Family: (Top) Dave, Ed & Jeff (Bottom) Joe & Edith.
▼

www.ingramcontent.com/pod-product-compliance
Lightning Source LLC
Chambersburg PA
CBHW070758050426
42452CB00012B/2390